CLOCK OF CLAY

OTHER BOOKS BY ROBERT HAZEL

POEMS

Poems, 1951–1961
American Elegies
Who Touches This
Soft Coal

NOVELS

The Lost Year
A Field of People
Early Spring

CLOCK OF CLAY

NEW AND SELECTED POEMS BY
ROBERT HAZEL

1992

LOUISIANA STATE UNIVERSITY PRESS
BATON ROUGE AND LONDON

Manufactured in the United States of America
First printing
01 00 99 98 97 96 95 94 93 92   1 2 3 4 5
Designer: G. Phoebe
Typeface: Granjon
Typesetter: G & S Typesetters, Inc.
Printer and binder: Thomson-Shore, Inc.

Library of Congress Cataloging-in-Publication Data
Hazel, Robert.
    Clock of clay : new and selected poems / by Robert Hazel.
        p.   cm.
    ISBN 0-8071-1738-2. — ISBN 0-8071-1739-0 (pbk.)
    I. Title.
PS3515.A9795C57   1992
811'.54—dc20   91-33749
                                                              CIP

Several of the poems in this volume have been published previ-
ously, sometimes in a slightly different form. "Consider the
Lilies" appeared originally in *Vortex,* and "The First Day of
Christmas" in the *New York Quarterly.* "Above a Trappist Mon-
astery," "Black Leather," "Celebration Above Summer," "Death
of the Farm Woman," "Indiana," and "Star" appeared originally
in the author's *Poems, 1951–1961* (Morehead University Press,
1961); "NYC" and "Who Touches This" in his *American Elegies*
(University of North Dakota Press, 1968); "Cow Salt" and "Let-
ter to the Kentuckian" in his *Who Touches This* (Countryman
Press, 1980); and "Health Education & Welfare Social Security &
Disability Office, Leesburg, Florida," "How It Feels," "On Miles'
Tribute to Duke," "Paragraph," and "Woman with Guitar" in
his *Soft Coal* (Countryman Press, 1985).

The paper in this book meets the guidelines for permanence and
durability of the Committee on Production Guidelines for Book
Longevity of the Council on Library Resources. ∞

TO
Albert Stewart

CONTENTS

CLOCK OF CLAY

CONSIDER THE LILIES

No clock strikes for a happy man.

How can I praise dandelions enough?
Even my tame azaleas amaze me

September cut down my father like a weed
He toiled not
Neither did he spin

Because these trees cannot walk
I wait for the Carolina moon
to stalk them before I shine
high as a white pine

A herd of trees cowed by a storm
I feel worms slide under the leaves to drink

A storm is what it wills
Leaves battered down
before the agreed rainbow

When it rains I take credit
I struck the rock

Shadows are friends
They know I hate the sun
for its injuries to me

Dreams hold night
The moon sheds pumice
into my eyes

Under a scythe-moon
deer & rabbits gnaw apples
under my midnight trees

The moon said: Look
at the cornfield
Silks rent sugar

Smooth in, little breeze
Time my skin
Crust my ears with pollen

4

A sweet small woman
slices peaches on a copper tray
Nobody will go hungry

My woman sucks the meat of artichokes
in olive oil & smells antiquity now

Maybe the wind will run away
Maybe it will be Sunday
& she shine like a fish

She laid leaves over the rotted spot
on my soul, succulent lips like aloe

At night she groins me
in a red house
Owls call softly
The parchment of our lives tears
& suddenly we are

Inside the womb
love will start
The embryo hears a heart

After you left
I held death by my hindered hand

Only fantasies tell us we loved

5
Here are sparrow nests
like rag dolls, so ugly
the straw falls beautifully out

The birds I hear sing
are dragons with wings & lice

A cardinal & his wife,
shavings of scarlet,
stitch twigs in a cedar
for two eggs

Opening his egg, my 3-yr-old cried,
"Daddy, it's the sun!"
Suffer the little children
I remind myself:
Before they die children
grow deeper than you

6
At dawn the cock's wattles
rhyme hens to huddle under
his yellow spurs

Violets anointed by dew play blue
I walk out into me

Eave water sorrows down
Dilated tulips tell the time
The implant of a dead star
in my bad eye

My white Leghorns fly down
at wheat time
I draw with fat kernels
the Christ star
& my birds form it
I draw David's star
& they form it
In a barnlot I create
from craw hunger
patterns of history I ken

7

Dreams are my perpetual terror
The dog rushes
I cannot move
to beat his skull
with an axe handle

A dog ran beside me
black like the space
between heart & spleen
Only by his dance I knew him
& chill overbare

Until I woke in terror
the dog had snarled
& circled in

8

I welcome all night sounds:
peeper frogs, alligator bellows,
limpkin shrieks, owls singing
courtship so softly who,
the strum of the banjo legs
of the wheewhiddlers

I hear these instinct cries
far from the terror of us,
us unable
& at dawn I draw in the hooked
blue catfish

Down on my hunkers below a sycamore
I hear a half-grown loud bird
demand insects
No matter how many times I salt
the birds' tails & pet them
I am ignored, I am nothing

At dawn lily lips speak
to the sun, their master
Today I cannot kill
Yellow is life's color

9
Ospreys scream then dive
like magnets for little fish

My legs break the tide
I tug the moon to Ireland

Waves lift & lower
Christ is my albatross

10
The cluttered cat chatters
her gleeful teeth at sight
of a robin on the lawn

I've seen animals shudder inside & out
while being slaughtered
I hear cattle low far as India

11

A death-bound moth touches
one antenna with the other
closing the circuit to light

A moth eats my wool
Should I read history?

12

I know no concepts
only bodies palpable to last touch
It is not being I understand
I suffered a haunt
in a clay graveyard

You fall far before
you open your eyes
to what you have dreamed
all your life
Before this moment
you were immortal

13

This stasis is memory
My knowledge of evil
is murder & suicide
going out & coming in
I have been shot at outside
Inside I have been cornered
in futile rage like Bacon's dog

What I hear by the sound
of my voice makes me tremble
for evil I have sprung

I speak no matter
only form a vortex
of joy for my voice
in chance to happen

14
I have no repining thoughts
that I deserve a better life
The sun gives me cancer & showers
& flowers & a stomach for fish
So, fat & sassy, I wear out nightmares
realer than waking hints of crazy

An orange light burns on water
What of the dark in my eyes?

Night has no dark for me
for all, all is darkness
in which I see

The more death I enclose within me
The more alive I become

15
Like an oyster its pearl
sanity hugs the insane
& singing to the mindless me
welcome without heed
sloth, terror, joy
as my heart chimes the hour
without knowing the year
Let me grovel in praise
in the basilica of my dreaming blood

PARAGRAPH

Beside New River I walked alone & sat on a boulder
& let my feet fall into the rapid water. My mind
began to sway away. I sensed a creature near & saw
a new-dead deer by the lone rock, its hindlegs in
the white froth current waving like a metronome.
I felt no shock. It was a time before thought was
invented to measure years, days, hours—no tick
of the human. Before religions, before any space
between life & death. In my quiet breath I was
some thing that simply was—without meaning,
the deer, the water, the sky, me before I became
myself. I thought nothing. Everything was for granted:
water into sky, deer into water, flesh on rock.

WOMAN WITH GUITAR

for Jan T. Randolph

Brown are the grasses of August
The animals fall & drowse
Sweet is the scent of dried blood

Fish leap into rock castles
Cast down your eyes like pebbles
deep in the pool of your body
where the next plucked string can ripple

Over your autumn guitar
you curve a waning moon
after the sun dives down
in raspberries & wine

Weave these notes on your fingers
like a girl's cats-cradles:

Sing one for the flowers of midnight
that nobody ever sees
Sing one for the touching of tongues
Sing one for the fret of your spirit

Go to the power, lost lover,
Sing father & mother in absence
your girlhood sunk in a ritual
of bells in Pennsylvania

Strum a boychild lost & furious
Chord the stench & ache of Washington
& the fever of loneliness

Time is the measure of mercy
Small is the acre of death

NYC

1

Gray to the marrow, pale as tall smoke
across the East River
the boneyard of Queens burns

Into my window charred letters fall
from the grim incinerators,
some still legible, with lovers' initials

and the brown reek of fire

2

Pools of blue children under the haze
under the sailing hats of nuns

3

Private darkness strays into rubble
where the Catholic god and the Jewish god
grow weak stems in cinders

Terror is private
A woman is murdered in 38 windows

Everybody is nobody's keeper
Ask mercy of stray cats

The dim roar of traffic over bridged boroughs
comes savage and sad

4

On an island staked out by stolen car aerials
professional liars in glass canyons cross
Madison Avenue and disappear
in secret Connecticut

Marcantonio's city of shattered wine bottles
and brown cut flesh rings Columbia in

In the midnight streets I hear
young whores cursing

5

The smiling girl who committed suicide,
mistress of gem thieves, hid a black eye
under Polaroid glasses

She screamed the length of her lover's coffin
She rode in a Cadillac long as a whore's dream

Lover, tell me the best hate
Murderer, tell me the best love

6

The cold wind shines

A train clicks quietly under the iron grating
where, with axle grease on a lead sinker,
a coatless man fishes for lost coins

I watch raw-knuckled care for all trivial, all small
And here

7

Banks whisper money
Male whores reply
Oiled locks slide free

8

Aluminum trucks bleat like lambs,
hauling barrels, crates over the cobbles
Streets grow long with vegetables and messengers

Near dawn I walk among fishnets and boatloads of coffins

And where the streets move, treeless,
I hear pawnshop trumpets

9

The ferry rides under gulls crying
in high monotones the water's given names
over Crane's forgotten bones

And wrecks passed without sound of bells

Acropolis builders, stand with me here, see how you failed!

INDIANA

North from Louisville
The window blind is brown
in my window night
falls from a tower
holding a clock
across the river a city
glows, and beyond
fields of winter wheat
church spires and silos
bodies measure shadows
no words are heard

the rented room is quiet
the Ping-Pong game in the hall
stopped at eleven
the pale girls have gone
to the White Castle
here silence is like
Dreiser dead, with a landlady
bent over his corpse
while her radio plays "Stardust"

I never draw the blind
whenever light comes
I do not want to miss it
light is my profession
it accustoms me to nights
when rats chew orange peels
in the waste can near my desk,
and I stand at the window
where smoke from the flues
settles blue on the pane
the bridge looks handwritten
I draw my initials
the way you trace your identity

when you are not thinking
where my hand has rubbed,
light, not my name, comes through

Harrodsburg: The Cemetery
The highway runs ahead of my injured eyes,
seeing only the concupiscent angels frozen:
the intuitive shame of motionless things,
the absence of consciousness and memory in the permanent grin
praise comes without honor, death without dignity;
the finite insult of prayers
takes no account of the distances
a live hand tapped electrically
in a red brick station against a green hill

an ingenuous painting might show a steam engine
    and gondolas paralleling a river
as on a Ping-Pong table in a basement
a group of women suggests patience
while town clocks measure the distances
from railyard to courthouse to coal-bucketed kitchens

but nowhere is the recognition that love or grief can be real

Indianapolis
The policeman's whistle is clear and thin
at the white island of monuments on Meridian
Street, weighted with tableaux of frontiersmen:
Clark in green bronze, sword drawn,
leans towards Vincennes, and pale green
water booms from the fountain
and settles to a stillness under the reign
of blue-and-gold state banners on aluminum
poles that face the tarnished Capitol dome
above six Corinthian pillars; the limestone

wilderness stretches, treeless, to the open
arcade of the bus terminal, a slam
of light down Market Street to the Harrison
Hotel, under a long red-and-white sign

gamblers with dry faces and sallow skin
ravel in the weaving walk of equal blacks with brown
expectations; the Circle Theater kills time
with a film based on a Lloyd C. Douglas novel shown
in Technicolor; and under his white helmet a modern
gladiator from North Vernon
creates Speed, a flying
red horse stenciled on the blue racer's engine,
while at the roller rink caryatids in
flesh-colored stockings support the roof, go nowhere in a din
of lucky wheels; on stage at the burlesque, near the wing
an Irish boy sings "Mandalay"; a bronze woman
with torch, on the monument's peak, faces south down Meridian

Bloomington

The same way prayers end,
letters always begin:

Dear Myself,
                              Today
I heard music, drowned
in sunlight and slaughterhouse blood
and a strange sense of rubber
tires rolling around
the speedway without cars
or drivers, because tonight
after Hoagy Carmichael went back
to the piano in the gym
and Wendell Willkie returned
to the Law library
my father called me in

from a war to put on the earphones
and listen to Berlin
I had to listen then
because tomorrow everybody
would be in our attic,
my father's workshop,
to listen to the first
shortwave receiver in town
and hear the romantic music
of Central Europe as if
it were one inch away
in Berlin a band was playing
from under the workbench
the color-coded wires
sped into the world

Milan

In the darkened houses
they watch television
Their walls are scrolled
with Christian mottoes in red wool

Coal piles by the railway
are dense and odorless

The county held the world's record
for corn yield per acre

Mechanical cornpickers stand like giraffes
Sheep make few night noises

Clocks are meaningless

Before a train arrives the switchblock
obeys a steel instinct for direction

No lives are suddenly sidetracked
Loss is criminal

A black standpipe wears
orange letters: STATE CHAMPS, 1954

Young cars ease to macadam
and accelerate with sexual squeals

The green glass of bottles
broken in the street

looks American

When Dreiser wrote he had no readers
When Willkie ran he got few votes

My cousin in bluejeans wept for Dean
and raced her Chevy the wrong way

down all the one-way streets
in search of ice cream

I did not suggest she go to a doctor
Who is insane?

Labels are dead wonders

Who is free? I had a gray jacket
too tight across the back

I strained against force,
my life confronted by perfect deadness

as I lifted the canvas mailbags
with brass padlocks, thrown from trains

I like to stand in the icy cones
of trains diminishing towards morning

It is not yet dawn
There is not enough light

CELEBRATION ABOVE SUMMER

Hear dark the priestly insects of my endless summer coast down to cells of
    wax,
and kind weeds bend my flowers to their colors' end;
in my thin acres hear time burn stones deaf
and radium's fine ticking to my flaunted ironweeds' blooms
stop in amazement at rough measures, twined of handclasps
and the rule of hammer-bruised thumb;

                              wonder and stature
of young celebrations shot from the dark earth build silent
my endless prism of rusted axes and fruit jars glowing with fireflies;
and curled in the quiet speculation of clods, my black calf,
sweet and voluminous, hooves maggoty in stiff air, columns high
the buzzards sailing;
                        O see my land turn back,
my summer ponds waved with cattle, my ironweed candelabra burning,
my knotted chickens, sure claws austerely clamped and dawn-triggered
to sweet August branches, sap-crested, wild and immune;
O hear my crony leaves measure fine spaces, inviting the brisk moon-stares
to shout out clear reeks under green flies, beautiful calf!
your magnificence sickens me with love;

see my slat gates nailed back to the green yawn of grass; see, under sour
    water,
mosaics of mint, and my country run
back everywhere green, green

ABOVE A TRAPPIST MONASTERY

A hand taking food beyond silence through an iron door glitters with fish
    scales;
beyond these purities thin sleet squeezes life from lambs in a hard winter;

in this world of wool and horns, my fathers,
tobacco leaves in blue cuffs, lean to fevered children;
and a young woman behind a coal bucket, hands in her ringed lap, dreams
    clear madonnas,
in her womb a new dead child;

fathers, be quiet, devoted, weave careful shawls for Clovis;
hide time in history;
in your silences
existence stands darkly before being;
in your renunciations
be not only clear but radiant
at the grated window, the shut door;
contain the furious germ;
pray that you kill no one;

from your city of mathematical lines,
full of varieties, successions, contrivances,
look at the lewd friezes of my vegetation;
inside the black sunflower stalk see the stillborn child;

when ice dripping to the flagstones uncovers
small bird skulls in your stone eaves,
look at my carrion land where winter lambs melt like hailstones
and be awed; curse and forgive the dead passion; absolve
this clay that takes no apocryphal wings!

fathers, during your daring and incredible silences I speak on,
washing your houses when you turn to dream;

though I did not attend her funeral,
I saw her many nights in shallow sleep;

I fished among ferns, eons of leaves, carp skeletons in limestone;
I sent her from the earth only all the leaves, lambs' hooves and fossils of
   children who cry killing

BLACK LEATHER

in memoriam, James Dean

In the merciless sky of his warbled days and nights
clouds imitate dreams the way light poles totem
electric deaths in the sprinkling neon of jukes
over mail-order orphans in their crazy runs through
the wire wheels of motorcycles and the black leather
of shielded rampage, skyrocketed, pledged
by his last ride from California to Indiana
with his untrue Italian girl's yellow scarf tied
to his crash helmet, going to a dirt track's scrambled race
at a little fair, for a small prize, the cloth screaming
behind him from Pasadena to his new gasoline death
ignited in paper cups among roadside weeds and in lean dust
along the monotonous shoulders of a grim highway of corn
spears, his brain suddenly still with this wild love

COW SALT

for Henry Birnbaum

White the blocks stacked on the street
before a hardware store in Indiana, savory in the sun
Henry Birnbaum, *schön* as his peartree name,
asked what. I said, Cow salt.
He gave a New York weary shrug,
Cow salt? There's no such thing!

I bent & cradled the life-giver for
how many years of fertility—
O my rush deep into the green where
I set the salt!

I don't go anymore where it is hauled
stay miles & miles away from slaughter
It stalks me in dreams
Nor have I lately strolled on Avenue C
in New York City where Henry led   I fear
that little start to die

May I sit in your house, Hersh ben Simon, & see
on TV the Washington Redskins? And on
your walls all the books & paintings
Love is simple permission

Trailing no clouds of glory, we come . . .
our teachers dead: Whitehall & Cargill—
friends in the earth or rotting in silence
In this grim interim of breath
the beast-me whimpers, unslaked,
calling to an emotive runt
I have dragged experiences behind me
like a mean dog   It snaps

Surcharge on my spirit? Nobody here to pay
I'm not in society, but log hours haunted
in a womb of green ferns
I choose nothing   I'm untracked
Yet less love was laid on the line than mine
O I have been beautiful as October!
Who will pay the tax now on my blemishes?

And you, Henry, not your brain clean
as a nail nor often wisdom can
fence chaos at the border of your last haircut
Billy Kilmer could have told you better
or your father, mystic Simon, closing the Sabbath over
the East River
Reason? Forget Spinoza & Kant
rare archaic intoxicant   How many sober mornings
have you died trying to imagine a prayer
you cannot utter?

White on the street, the blocks of your disbelief
Lot's wife looked back, too

If the salt shall lose its savor
who will remember the sting
to my cut hand, to your blind eye
the first pain of holy?

SPECTRUM & SANDSTONE

to Harriet Sappé

Pale sky   Pale turf   Pale horse
Albert Ryder

Dead fish   Dead ferns   Dead talons
Morris Graves

Sandstone worn   Granules drifting   Cold animal
Flannigan

Rain on Chelsea   Rain on pigeons   Rainbow
Arthur Sappé

THE FIRST DAY OF CHRISTMAS

One turtle dove
two turtle doves
three turtle doves
in the hawks' talons
Come to NYU
Come to NYU
Be raped on Park Avenue
You girls of Forest Hills
come to NYU
Be raped in Washington Mews
Lie in your apartments
blood caked on your mouths
You girls of Virginia
come to NYU
Be raped in the Port Authority
your first night in the city
present your injury
in red hieroglyphics
to St. Vincent's emergency
Come to NYU
You girls from Vermont
come to NYU
Be raped in Macdougal Alley
Come get your comeuppance
Come to NYU
You girls of New Jersey
Come to NYU
Be raped in Sheridan Square

    Flail your Head
    left to right
    grit your teeth
    bite your tongue
    below a scream
    held in the talons

of a diving hawk
and beaten blue
Come to NYU

Any girl too dumb
to want to have some fun
deserves to be slapped
with the butt of a gun
Come to NYU
You girls from Carolina
come to NYU
be raped on Bleeker Street
get gonorrhea free
from the hawk's tail
Leave a blood trail
on a white towel
Thrash your head
to and fro
Come to NYU
The rapist is brief
furious he tears in
lays knife upon pillow
where you can see
He knocks out your teeth
Nothing you can do
Come to NYU
Loeb Student Center
NYU
One Jewish girl
One Jewish Girl
epitome of beauty
One Jewish girl
raped in Patchen Place
on the cobblestones
her body bruised and cut
concealed by makeup

Eyes on the floor
of Loeb Student Center
pills in her purse
ready to OD
feeling filthy all over
Gonna OD
Can't phone your parents
to tell them where you are
Who is so reckless as
to walk in Washington Square?
Can't tell her father
Can't tell her mother
Can't tell her fiancé
Gonna OD
One turtle dove
one cyanide
one cyanide
One turtle dove
screams in the talons
of a hungry hawk
One cyanide
pill will do
Bye little girl
Bye little girl
After you OD
I shall stand
on First Avenue
to see your hearse go by
out to Long Island
where you still shall lie
Bye, little Jew
I love you
One turtle dove
One singing wing
of one turtle dove

caught by a hawk
Feathers and blood

One turtle dove
One foreign trip
one trip to Europe
try to forget
but cannot forget
one painful cry
one bloody thigh
Endless foreign trip
sent by parents
to Switzerland
the remainder of your life
One turtle dove
one degradation
In Switzerland
you will remain
You can never regain
self or the knife
laid on your pillow
Invaded and thrown
you cannot return
Orthodontist can
replace your teeth
cracked on St. Mark's Place
but you cannot forget
and you cannot return
to the lazy swell
of a lordly day

Come to Fun City
Come to NYU
Get an audition
on how to break your spine

Come to NYU
Here in Bellevue
I can't see the sky
I live only because you
come to visit me
Ward NO-5 is lonely
The shrinks feed me pills
to sedate me
no psychiatric help
just the powerful downers
to wipe out Connecticut
where as a kid
I winked at fireflies
All night the crazies wail
I keep going only
because you visit me
One turtle dove
mad as Ophelia
singing her water songs
One turtle dove
caged for life
in Bellevue Nut Ward
NO-5
I tuck you under my wing
For you I sing
Silent white
Doric columns
Doric white
silent columns
Fluted stone Doric stands
Stately Bellevue
lost hospital
of NYU
One way in
No way out

of NO-5
Bellevue Nut Ward
silent and white

On the first day of Christmas
my sweet pets gave to me
All my pretty ones
gave to me
One turtle dove

ISLAMORADA

to Frances Whyatt

Don't need love
Need alcohol
Don't need touch
Need alcohol
Into alcohol
Never pour water
Water weakens
whoever you care
Don't need love
Love asks what it lacks
in the bars of next
Froth of the Keys
like tiaras on rocks
The white brine of gillnets
The tang of dead fish
Awash the shrill light
Fandango of palms
& my pure pilgrim
jumps coral after
Like a bird drifting
coos to her soul

Come back, come back

FOR THE FIRST DAY OF BENJAMIN

In the amniotic seas
where great sperm lured
Milton & Melville
a green bottle drifted
a note inside with your name

Your memorized gills dried
& suddenly trees for your eyes!
Dry land your fortune & curse
In the early dew of leaves
birds wave & dry their wings

A friend of your parents said:
I have doubt about bringing a child
into the world at this time
May this verse erase his innocence

All times are evil
from the first stone thrown
to the high-blown atom
glorifying Eden
In Japanese atom
is Original Child
Was life made safe
for Caesar or Gandhi?

"I see men as trees walking"
Below an angel wreathed
in chiseled stone laurel
I see a bird recline
& a woman slice an apple
& your arms, your reaching arms!
She hears the parlance of your body

The music of a truck horn
& headlights bloom
on the moon's blind side

STAR

for Frédéric Thursz

All day, higher than the heads of executioners,
the earth rose against the clean blades of bulldozers
and fell without echo at dusk on galaxies of bones:
the seedless bodies of bearded men, milkless women,
children with dark stars sewn on remnant clothing;
in the leaf-green country surrounding Dachau the discoverers
climbed down from the iron of their machines
and smoked on the raw mounds, mouth deep in bones

        At the end of history
           these
      were discovered dead:
         a victory
    over starvelings whose knees
          bled;
     the beauty of the head
        and eyes
  of a fly or a Jew, something to be
      crushed and buried
   at the beginning of history

On the iron crosses, on the claws of black eagles,
on the cold edges of the voices of young men,
on the shields of tanks and weapons carriers,
on the Bronze Age swastikas, on the tenons of oak tables
of knights in their tarnished lust married to violence,
on the Druid trees in wolf-toothed swamps, on wire cutters,
they were caught on the crosses, dismembered and killed

      In the darkest nights stars grow.
      Black threatens them, always.
      Some are clotted with red.

Some drift in the incandescence of the sky.
Some are goblets lifted, held for a moment
in a strange land

ON MILES' TRIBUTE TO DUKE

The whole hell is honey my bees strayed to
Flown are the dark larks of Carolina
   & the wired-puppet starlings of Harlem

John Wayne said God went thataway
I never caught up with those horse's asses
I'm still mired down in Baldwin & Florida
I'm not the American who killed the rooster
   that prayed for rain at 4:00 a.m.
   in Black Town
   where bitten dogs weep at dawn

Let the owl scowl
Count wandering armadillos
Count wild berries & busted bicycles
Count dark children as they wince over hot sand to the honey
   of a church organ, drums & hungry voices
   calling to a microfilm Jesus in the brain

HEALTH EDUCATION & WELFARE
SOCIAL SECURITY & DISABILITY OFFICE,
LEESBURG, FLORIDA

I thought she was stoned until I could see her eyes, then
I knew she was only quietly crazy, a black girl about 20
We stood in line together & whether I wanted to talk or not
    she settled that
What you name?   Robert   I be Wilhelmina
   & she took my hand in her fine hand, asked,
    You know what I had for breakfast, a glass of water
Her amber face tugged my attention
    like a fish on my line
She said at Sumter a doctor killed her first child
    by a forced abortion, but she had another
She said, My baby girl be 3 months old   She have no orange
    juice
She told me they had not eaten for 2 days now
People in line waiting for the office to open were staring
    at a white man & a black woman talking so much
These other Crackers avoided me, but how could I quit?
    Shit,
I've been hungry & will never get full   God, she was
    beautiful!
Still, I was surprised they let her out of Sumter Asylum to try
    to get work until I realized the attitude of the State
    was To Hell With This Black Girl
She said she will build a new life   O, yes! Until her eyes die
Her appeal for food for her & her infant daughter will go
under the office file of dead paper
As I leave, I lean over, touch her face & whisper
Make it, Momma, make it   Wilhelmina said, Mister Robert,
    take care

I did not say, Blue Lady, let loose & die
for justice & mercy never were meant for you

FOR EPHRAIM

Now a life is lifted from eons of water, fern & bone into the arms of East
    Instinct & West Light

I rejoice! Your birth swims love's blood

May the butterfly wind you in sunbright
May you never be caught in a riflescope
May ideology follow biology
Ideas will surface later to confuse you forever
May you learn skills as axiom, as your fathers advanced with wood spears
    toward their totemic brothers
May the owl, whose wings make no whisper, drop a torn squirrel at your
    feet to teach you how still death is
"We cannot prevent the birds of sorrow from flying over our heads, but we
    can prevent them from building nests in our hair"
May you be an adventurous boy who dives into cold Easter water to retrieve
    the Cross, so to make material your soul even as the young god was made
    flesh
May you leap & hop & be scratched & bleed & be patched up & be stung by a
    bee, for pain is the measure of joy

As you grow, may the odor of sweating girls obsess you
As you drift in the maelstrom of being, may a cold light burn to illumine
    you

DEATH OF THE FARM WOMAN

Same bones, same face, same hair
I touch now, after the embalmer

lying level body, tame to the dumb frame
of the metal trestle

Railway crossings and bus intersections
where you waved sons away, old woman

Went to bright town, pinched timid dimes
To cheap cafeterias we traveled, thought them rich

But our gardens, the fruit of!
sat paring apples after sundown

said for saying, word for word
in country, Mother of dandelions

How we ran! where the water found us, with me under your heart,
young startled girl, waiting for my eyes to open

Not any clod any weed any dry furrow any spraying weed
or clod's crumble, not any stick of wood wears your hand again

So easy, to lift you now on my eyes
as the sun changes

lift you above bronze handles of your casket, above plastic grass
to a green place, on your own dumb sayso

As you stay still here, breathless
in the presence of cedar,

clay to my clay,
your meadow arms hold silence to our stillest leaves

your love-dried lips, brought up with wax, do not say
You sew these ending stitches through my lips

LETTER TO THE KENTUCKIAN

to Wendell Berry

I

My earth announced by rising flocks of leaves
Under green a horse's veins strut on his running
Sunflowers bend east   Their tongues take summer's host
In the morning mist apple buds flare like candles

Here comes the sun to my magnet! Too much life!
I have bitten my mouth   I spit blood

In my mouth more than thirst for my own blood and the blood of other
    animals,
the holy mass of summer! yes
and I pray by waving a scythe at high grass

In one long rush of my breath
a dandelion's white head
bursts to tufted life

Fly, little wild birds! Handsome cock fathers, sing!

At the end of cut weeds and battered clods
    the kiss of water
    stigmata of sun-fired windows
    echo of walls
    silence of photographs
    patience of drowsing flowers

Fireflies light their day   Cells settle   Sugar seeps
I hear the scrolls of corn stop unwinding
    and the birds stop reading them,
    tuck head under wing

I have my own twiggy dreams—
To town where carnival birds
    fly on whistling sticks

Weave a circle round me

I'm dizzy   I'm lucky   I'm magic!

And I can step in any river twice

2

Your hard hurt bring me   your unread books your wrong
eyeglasses your illegible letters your relief checks used car
payments your hard hurt hearts bring me   your death insurance
bring me faceless documents printed in code dealt you for inked Xs
and usury   your hard hurt times bring me   your bruised hands
porkfed weakness green vomited mornings your lardassed lovelings
bring me your dry faces dry gardens dry batter your dull senses
your hick brains your helpless hands your slat backs having bent
over your already done work bring me your grinning brown tobacco
mouths your loud laughter you fools! you fools before bankers and
sheriffs O weak weak and hurt hard by your dires hurt blue and
so sadly go inferior clumping into general stores go rummaging
in black back pockets for dimes among bent nails and twine go
let the townsmen take the dangling buttons off your Sunday coats
pluck lint from the chains of old slow watches and other
poor white and black bone and metal cold now in their
candied town hands

3

Crossing the Ohio
where my homeland breaks at the river
to an orchard of tombstones
beside the superhighway
where engines sing in anger

under a neon frieze
of hamburger and beer stands
I have come to gentle you, Old Ones,
to soothe you like colts with my hands
carry whispers like wheat to your corpses

Old Ones, honor me now
Your bones decorate my wrists
Dead children swindle my arms
In the exile of recall
From the hourglass full of spiders
return me your sweet hearts

Yes, Mother, your pulse sobs
over a hip-carried child
Father, your serious eyes!
Yes, look me straight in the face

Dead blood turns black
Grief is a way to turn
But who can see tears in the rain?
I gaze at your flowers of lime
I call these stones by your names

4

White scales the house   The painter is dead
Green binds the house   The trimmer is dead
Hands search the house   The lovers are dead

5

A gone world, ours   Once upon a time

Our chronic dirt, hick curiosity, boys' blood,
our hands cut to the quick
bled like the sawed-off horns of cattle

from sharp tools our fathers thrust into our ribs
before we were old enough to shave

Learning was pain
during the first terror and failure
But what elation to discover
we could pinch, pry, jimmy, jack
a world into place!

After we knew sunsets
fierce as the severed head of a horse,
washed the crusted blood from our foreheads,
took pleasure no longer in killing,
learned how to smile at wives and children
and nod our willing heads to hairy sod,
dream smooth dreams,
not shouting fear and rage,
learned not to attack the already wounded,
but kiss eyes, hair, faces of sufferers
and care for all suddenly young and torn

What meaning now? Virtues?
Repeat Colonial tales of common acts and faith?
Green people, green rivers?
Devoted builders, defiant to kings for sake of us,
bringing fire to our hearths?

Who, if we shouted, would hear us in the drive-in theater?
We have seen used-car bumpers welded into sculpture

WHO TOUCHES THIS

to Walter Freeman

Every time I dream, I am alive
Every time I remember a dream,
I know I have lived

Mother, lie
Father, rise

I live in the mountains and work the farm
my father and I cleared and kept green
I hear a creek bubble loud like my heart
and thrushes' wings whisper over the hill
I meet my boyhood on a gravel road
and see how beautiful I was then
honey Robert me

Dreams! My skull explodes with dreams
like the white heads of dandelions
I sit in a room in Manhattan
hearing empty bottles fall,

savage words in other windows,
the gears of a garbage truck
I live in the pain of my father
who tried to cross his hands
when he choked and choked
when the last stroke struck

If I have no way to go
that way is good
I am learning how not to live
I shall forget every valuable thing
last and first forget the woman
I said love to said love said love

I will tell you a bitter thing, blind heart:
the wild ways you have perfected
the way hunters create the life of a deer with knives

The purpose of learning is to forget before you die
But a man must try to learn something unspeakable,
    something that makes him tremble

The lone black man
in this gritty precinct
of flower children
woke me at 4:00 this morning
crying, "Whore of Babylon!"
Near sleep I heard something
perfect as a dream
so certain that I felt
it would survive my waking
It was only the hoarse
repetitions of a drunk man
shouting, cursing, weeping
how this nation was killing
all his innocent children
Yet strangely when he stood
pounding the garbage cans
and imploring, "America!"
the word sounded beautiful
as if he believed it

I have become my face
My face smiles for me
on public occasions
when a man's peers
are all photographers
Then at 5:00 p.m.
I return to an old vacancy
called my heart

And where will you speak, Robert,
after 5:00 p.m., and to whom?
Tell a dimestore mirror
how you have loved
father & mother, brothers & sister
and a woman from Brooklyn?
God, drag these loves
at the end of a leather halter
like the dead cats and dogs
I dangled as a child
at the end of a dusty rope
before they begin to stink!

I have written this in a ring-binder
that belonged to a friend who cut his wrists
There is a smear of blood on the cover

It is nearing dawn
This is the way I say no to God
and the way God laughs back at me
in the cold shirt of my skin

HOW IT FEELS

I could say how it feels bereft of friends loved
This is dangerous because I could honor death utterly
I could throw away dice & cards & the Complete Shakspere
This is dangerous because I could forget pain's amnesty
I could tear up photos of women whose faces are the braille of weary
& discard tintypes of men with hard eyes who nested me on their black vests
I could become a sad child again & parade my hunger like a string of
  sunfish
This is dangerous because dark might smother the seedbed
& I'd forget to hate the crow & the cutworm that flies in the night

I could even think it's important to stay alive
I could forget to throw this away

CLOCK OF CLAY

Be this as I may
   thirsty, red-eyed, fresh out of honey,
   pitiful & wrong
   a liar & tonguer of puke
I cannot think about what I am thinking
   or know what I'm knowing next
I did not think this out
It came to me all of a sudden
   like the scream of a whore being beaten in Ironton
Became a rager
Became rotten by faith in hymens
Fouled oven, green spewed potatoes,
   green dotted crusts in the breadbox,
   lumps of mold in the grape jelly jar,

To revive from death each morning
   with a sexual urge defying this latest suicide
& see the schefflera plant kicked over
   soil inextricable from the carpet
Aspirin reminds me my friend has cancer
   & yet God has not said a word
   even though this is Sunday
Melon rinds on the kitchen floor
Magnificent cockroaches with amber wings
   scurry for hideouts
My head does not throb for conscience
I insulted nobody

I begin to live subterranean
   downy with sick wishes
Hurry to hang up the phone on pretty New Yorkers,
   friends dear & nervous who have never pissed on grass
Voice of my body speaks in high tones of disease

Many sweetnesses will go down with me that were never spoken
    & nobody else could or ever will
Delicate willings will die on my fruitful hands
There will be no trellis in the garden of my bones
    to train them up to sun
I send these to you undone
I have been the hermit bee of all sweetness

I have no future   The river
    is flowing backwards
My past is my present
& I retort to Charcot, Freud, Husserl
    Binswanger, Heidegger, Buber
    You tone-deaf piano tuners
    who wanted me to become what I never wanted to be!
I am becoming nothing

Melancholy & fear of heights are part of becoming
I have that sense of being crushed, bones & muscle

I am the man who cannot exceed himself
Threnody is my name

Who is the doctor?
Who is the patient?

Now I echo the shadow that I am
Losses chain me & I'm stuck in the mud,
    the dirt of death on my hands
& the world shrinks to my cowboy sombrero
    when I was green as an ideal twig,
when I sang while milking cows & flooded cats' pink mouths
    with white comets from lavish teats
I am only a reed, the weakest reed in nature
    but I am a thinking reed

Things break away like brown tendrils
    down a lattice of roses
Stand under the spire
Christ isn't there
    only a dead Jew my people pray to

By praying to a dead god you have insulted me
Let not any god nor human law diminish me
The spire holds against hell & is beautiful
    all the way from Roma to Constantinople
Everything falls away
    down a trellis of brown roses
Take this poltice of hope, these fat green leaves
    off my eyes!
& the spiraling red veins of the embryo
O, galaxy of life that bears
    the bronze stars of dead light!

Hungry as a child, leave a pie on the sill
    & I'll eat it & lie about it
    if I get whipped equal to what dies inside me
    If you grew up poor, there is nothing like
        a bean sandwich or sucking a raw egg in the barnloft

The dirty earth hides me
The sane man ditches around his house like Noah
But my god turned out to be a eunuch
    on a throne of wax
When lightning struck, the little god melted down
    along with candles & buttermilk
We searched for the blind kittens under the porch
    only to kill them with a kind hammer

Sycamores drink the Wabash of Dresser, Dreiser, Porter,
    Skelton & Carmichael, true

What am I made of?
The sweet water of limestone Indiana
The weight of rain, snow, sleet, mud & manure
Very well, how do you smell me,
my colleagues in universities?
I shall put white pockets on white trousers
    & die of Lucky Strikes
    before you discover

Mosquitoes don't fly in rain
    so I can bait my hooks for blue catfish
New River girl, the glossy boys tailing
    didn't find you
I'd give up my front seat in hell
    to teach you how to make love

I'm at the bottom of the barrel:
    feet infected, blood sugar high, no energy,
    legs so weak I couldn't take a bale of hay
    from a pissant
Nur wer die Sehnsucht kennt
However, beloved brother,
as we go down, as we turn down
    to a lettered stone
as we go down
Drink up   Drink up!

Little boons swarm my face
to probe for blood & leave itch
    & experienced spiders leave a red spot
    on my pillow
    to remind me who's boss

I run a treadmill
level with evil—no gain into good

Experience is no help
I must do it all over
Now is the time of night sweats
   & wakeful despair
far from playing football & drinking milk
   instead of alcohol
My head rims into the helmet
   dented & scarred by wishes of heroism

I hear the click of a Japanese camera
   on Keats' sedges

The High-Rafter-Bat politician said
at the convention they had hippies, gays & way-out people
They had some long-haired sonofabitch singing
   The Star Spangled Banner
   & he was so drunk he didn't even know the words
   He must have been some smartass Liberal
His wife reminded him:
   You don't even know who Willie Nelson is

The leather glans penis dangles
The blue frog lashes in a fly

Once I circled with my arms
   orchards, groves & vineyards
I was rich with pure lust
   for all clods, shoots & sprouts
Now I am only a grain of dust
I have been to a strange land
   & met the dark man

My mother was a virgin bride
& I'm her first son, her prince
But I'm the stupidest man ever
   in my veins running carousals

On the human train I'm the caboose
Even God could not set a dove on my head

Great-Uncle Bob's house in Jennings, Florida,
had no screens against mosquitoes
where he died insane
I'm named for him   Bless me, for you could not sin
He was called like Isaiah to dispute the priests of Baal
Having no oxen to lay upon a pyre, he shot rabbits,
laid them upon chestnut rails & prayed mightily
No fire came from heaven
Betrayed by God, undone
He walked from Indiana to Florida
He lived on yams & peanuts from a small garden
until, caved in, he happily invaded hell

After the priest told her she was wed
the little girl in her hippie tattered long white dress
& barefoot came down all the aisles
& hugged us each one by one honestly
That child's heart was surely placed

In the final direction of the elementary town
    spartan children of Appalachia advance
    whipped & bed-wetting
With my axe they crack the multicolored dome
    of a terrapin
They kick dogs & yank the tails of cats
    until they spit
They eat raw turnips, suck eggs & smoke Camels

The last shall never be first
Beaten from birth, they will shudder
    in the leather straps of an electric chair

Clouds wind over small grim houses
They shudder in high near fear of tornadoes
Even cats are afraid to kill, their first joy gone

Sores, eruptions, melanomas, burnt flesh
    & a surgeon saying I am to buy back my life
    if I give up the inhalation of blue smoke

My life has been lived at night
    in the chemistry of dark slavery
Before my life is reinvented by tubes
    in imitation of the living cord
I shall cut free

After you do the first thing
the second thing is go down to the water

I have come to hate my life
    revealed in nightmares
    schizophrenic by night
    in the handcuffs of language by day
Often the damned know without being taught
I swear on a family Bible whose binding
    is the hide of a redskin
In a way destruction is happy because everything
    seems the same
Man in his maggot warren insists nothing is wrong
as long as there is ice cream & an emperor

Often I lie down & dream
or take the revenge of sweethearts
    who went next, simple

It would be arrogance to think I could lose anything
My memory is so poor that it is always losing & finding
    the same haunts

To stand up, you have to be able to fall down

I'm alone & glad of it
A time comes when a man gets shut of himself

Priestly & hollow I stand on this ground
of names from England & Germany
I sit on a throne of straw
heaped up by raw men & women
    with wrinkles like iron filings

Know, Thou
    the arterial fertile trails red as a cock's comb
    on a ridge of sycamores
Know, Thou
    the evenings of lovely lust
Know, Thou
    Hinder no heart its wash & weave red sluice
Love, Thou, at once
Love, Thou, excessively

Clock of clay
I sit by the seacoast of Bohemia
Sturdy beyond belief, white marbles
    lie to linger forever
Under the seal's wide spindrift gaze
Silurian stones dream of eyeless peace